Real Estate Investing Blueprint For Beginners

How To Create Passive Income On Properties
To Escape The Rat Race And Reach
Financial freedom

Table of Contents

Introduction

The following chapters will discuss everything that you need to know when you are ready to become a landlord and earn money on your very own rental property. There are a lot of great investment opportunities that you can choose from. But there is nothing that is quite like working with real estate. And when you choose to invest your money in a rental property, you could easily earn a nice profit each month if you find good tenants and keep up with properties with good maintenance.

This guidebook is going to take some time to explain all of the things that you need to know to get started with your first rental property. We will discuss the importance of financial freedom and how real estate investing, especially with rental properties, will be able to help you to reach those goals of financial freedom.

From there, we are going to dive right into the process of searching for and finding the perfect rental properties for your needs. We will look at how you can look for a property, how to get the right financing, the importance of doing an analysis on the property, and even how to determine your return on investment to determine if you are actually going to be able to earn an income on all of the work that you do.

In the final section, we are going to discuss what you will need to do when you actually own the property. We will look at how to find the right tenants, how to maintain and fix up the home, how to collect rental payments, and even how you may work with a property manager to help you get the income, without having to be there and help your tenants all of the time.

Getting started in rental properties is going to take some time, dedication, and so much more. But for those who are looking for a good way to increase their financial freedom, and who want to be able to own their own time, then this is one of the best investment opportunities for you to go with. When you are ready to get started with your own rental property investment, make sure to check out this guidebook to help you out!

There are plenty of books on this subject on the market, thanks again for choosing this one! Every effort was made to ensure it is full of as much useful information as possible, please enjoy!

Chapter 1: Real Estate Investing for Beginners

Investing in real estate is another method of putting your money to work today and allowing it to grow and multiply as time goes. For the investment to be worthwhile, though, the 'returns' or the 'profits' you get from your investment must be able to cover the taxes imposed on the property, the maintenance cost, insurance, the risks taken, and the costs of other utilities.

The concept of investing in real estate is quite simple. First, it requires a basic understanding of the nature of the investments economics involved and the risks you will be bear when you invest. To make a profit, you must invest in properties, collect rent, and manage the money you get so that you can invest it in other businesses as well. Note that 'simple' does not mean that the real estate business is 'easy.' It is marred with risks—ranging from minor to large disasters that could make you lose your property or even worse.

Although there are risks involved, real estate investment remains one of the most popular and most lucrative investment ventures because of its straightforward approach. The business comprises a fair exchange between a property owner and the property user. As long as the user pays rent and as long and as long as the owner ensures that his property remains safe and with a proper connection (electricity and water, although the renter pays the bills), the deal is sealed. However, there may be added complexities depending on the type of real estate investments such as commercial, industrial, residential, and the kind that trades on stock exchanges called REITs.

Ways That Real Estate Investors Make Money

There are four ways to make money on the real estate vehicle:

Cash Flow Income

This is the kind of real estate investment where a person purchases or constructs an apartment building and starts collecting rent from renters, thereby creating a stream of income in the form of rent. Rent is the amount of money that a tenant pays to a landlord to use their property for a specified period, usually, a month. Examples of spaces to rent include office buildings, car washes, some storage units, rental houses and apartments, and others.

Appreciation of Value

When the value of real estate property goes up due to changes in the market, it creates profits for the owners. For example, suppose a large mall is built next to your land, your land will become busier and scarcer because more people will be wanting to use it to create businesses that support the mall such as running a parking lot. Anything you construct there, such as apartment buildings, will be more attractive to renters and buyers than it could have been if the facility was not there.

Supplementary Investment Income

Real estate investing is an excellent source of supplementary income that comes from facilities like the laundry facilities installed in the low-income apartments and vending machines erected in office buildings. Facilities like these are similar to mini-businesses, and they help to supplement your income by providing services and products that your collection of customers will need.

Real Estate-Related Income

This is the income enjoyed by the real estate 'specialists,' the brokers, who make money through the commissions they receive when people sell or buy real estate property. There are also real estate management agencies employed to collect rent from tenants. Companies like those earn money by charging a commission for the rental income received. For example, a real estate company is hired to manage the daily operations in a hotel. The company might be allowed to take 5 percent of all sales, in exchange for running day-to-day operations like running the receptionist desk, hiring maids, washing the towels and mowing lawns.

The reality is that the majority of us will not get rich and attain financial independence by merely doing our jobs. One of the reasons is that the time we dedicate to work each day is not enough to achieve any tangible success. The much that many can do is feed, clothe and shelter themselves. They will afford luxuries like cars and vacations, but these will require them to bend their backs every day working.

For us to be financially independent, we need to come up with multiple streams of passive income. Passive income is income that you earn without needing to be physically present. Smart real estate investment is one of the ways to do this, for big returns with relatively low risks.

Investing in real estate can appear challenging although it is not. You only need to wrap your mind around some important basics before you dip your foot.

Real Estate Investment Types

Rental Property Investing

The most popular and common form of real estate investing is residential real estate. It includes investing in condos, single-family houses, and townhouses. These houses are built to be rented out or sold at a profit. For example, as an investor, you can buy a condo that is near the beach at $100,000 then rent it out on Airbnb for $100, and you will make a lot of money from it.

Large residential properties are those that are intended for use by businesses, and they often are categorized as commercial real estate. Owners of buildings like these make money from renting out office space or from renting out multi-family residential units. There is a rule that indicates that residential buildings that have more than 4 units should be classified as commercial buildings. A commercial-residential house will follow different lending criteria when it comes to the mortgage terms and conditions.

When trying to identify a good rental property, there are many factors you need to keep in mind. The first is that you will want to limit your search to neighborhoods that have low crime rates, well-rated schools, strong employment figures and those whose value is appreciating.

Once you have narrowed down your search to a particular area or specific properties, you should then run some calculations to see the prospects of those properties generating some income for you. The goal here is to find a property that will bring in a positive cash flow such that the rental income you earn is higher than the expenses you incur. It should cover the repairs, insurance, mortgage payments, property taxes, and management fees.

Another way to do this is to take up the 1% rule. This rule is used to determine whether some property is viable for investing in or not. Applying this rule, you took the estimated monthly rental income and divided it by the purchase price. If the figure you get is 1% or ranges just about there, then you can be sure that you have an excellent rental property.

For example, let's say you intend to purchase a property at $400,000 and you estimate the monthly income to be $4500 (assuming that there will be no vacant houses). Then using the 1% rule, divide the $4500 by $400,000 and you will get 1.13%, which should tell you that the property would be a viable investment.

One of the challenges of investing in rental property is the number of expenses involved. Before committing yourself to them, make a list of all possible costs. If you fail to include even one expense upfront, you will have an inaccurate estimate of the costs and consequently, of the income you expect.

The list of expenses is long, and it includes things like broker commissions, mortgage fees, repairs, maintenance and cleaning, advertising to tenants, insurance, utilities, property management, mortgage interest, legal fees, the cost of replacing broken down appliances, taxes, tax-return preparations, and legal fees. You also ought to factor in the time and the expenses you will cover to get you back and forth the property.

It is close to impossible to know for sure how much of each expense your investment will take. Therefore, as you prepare to make your investment in the rental property business, ensure, first that you gather as much information as you can, both from owners of similar properties, from tenants and real estate agents. Make sure also to make provision for any unforeseen costs.

Commercial Trade Estate

Commercial real estate refers to property that is exclusively used for commercial purposes. It includes property that serves as offices, restaurants, stores, malls, and industrial parks. Businesses and companies typically lease these spaces to maintain flexibility and cost-effectiveness.

The profitability of commercial real estate should surprise you. It is interesting to find out that McDonald's gets the majority of its profits from its property assets and not from food, despite being one of the most popular fast food companies in the world. It owns property in some of the most premier locations in the world.

Some businesses may own the space they use, but the majority has to pay rent and leases for the space they occupy. A lease runs from between one year to 10 years. Large tenants take longer leases while small businesses take relatively shorter leases. A short-term lease allows the owner more flexibility in terms of adjusting the lease rent, but the long-term ones provide security.

Commercial property is categorized into three classes. Class A is made up of property that is rated among the best in terms of age, aesthetics, location and the quality of the structure. Class B buildings are those that are older but are not competitive as class A buildings in terms of their prices. These buildings are sort after by investors who want to flip them. Class C buildings are those that are very old, usually more than 20 years. They are located in the lesser attractive areas and need maintenance.

Investing in commercial real estate can be lucrative and act as a good hedge against the market's volatility. Investors can reap massive profits from appreciation, but the majority of the returns they will get through rental income collected from the tenants.

In most cases, the properties are sold as entire buildings like an office building, a restaurant, or a factory. However, if an investor wants to reap more returns from the deal or hopes to see the profits more quickly, he ought to break down the project into smaller units rather than sell it as a whole.

Flipping Houses

Flipping is a term that was coined in the United States to refer to the practice of purchasing an asset that generates revenue and then quickly reselling it at a profit. As such, flipping houses is the practice of a real estate investor buying houses, then selling them at a profit. When you buy a house with the intention of flipping it, you must be ready and equipped to sell it quickly. The time between the purchase and sale can only be a maximum of one year.

There are two kinds of house flipping:

a) An investor purchases a house that has the potential to increase in value once the structures are repaired and updated. Once the work is done, the investor sells the house for a higher price than was purchased.

b) An investor purchases a property whose value is rising rapidly. Here, no updates are made. The investor only holds the property for some months before reselling it at a higher price, thus making a profit.

House flipping, when done right, is a great investment vehicle because in only a short time and with only small repairs or renovations, you can reap so much more than you paid for it. However, the flip can quickly go the other way. Some people purchase houses and later find that the foundation of the house is shaky or that the roof is leaking. Fixing these issues could cost too much money, or not be worth doing at all, and in the end, you could lose a lot of money.

Ways to Flip Houses with Success

1.   Use cash to finance the house flip.

House flipping is double-edged; it could succeed or go south. This makes it unreasonable to add to your debt when flipping the houses. If you choose debt, you increase your costs because you will have to pay interests for it for some months, which increases the price to be charged to ensure that the investor breaks even. A highly priced house could take time to sell.

Financing the flip using debt money could cause you to be desperate and act out of desperation because if the house has stayed a while, you may be tempted to lower your prices, which will eat into your profits.

2.   Study the market.

Many flippers get excited about their next project and may forget to study the current market performance. Without a clear understanding of the market, you could experience a number of issues. For one, you will not have an idea of whether you are getting a good deal on the house you intend to buy or not. Ideally, you should only buy a property for 80% of its value, then subtract the costs of the repairs.

Without proper market knowledge, it will also be impossible for you to assess the value of the property and its potential value accurately. The vision you have for the home should also fit into the reality of the neighborhood you are buying into, such as their ability to afford the house you are pursuing.

Lastly, without adequate market knowledge, you will have difficulties pricing the house. For example, if the house range in a particular neighborhood is 130k to 150k, you need to work out a plan so that the price you bring to the market after flipping the house is on the lower end of that range.

3.   Have a budget for the house you intend to flip.

Make a budget even before you purchase the home taking in the cost of the property, the repairs, and marketing it.

4.   Focus on the smaller renovations.

Investors have big dreams for their projects, such as hardwood floors, trendy light fixtures, and professional-grade stoves, among others. However, if you focus on doing grand things like these, the budget could quickly get out of hand. A budget beforehand will help to keep track of the updates while ensuring that you up the value of the house.

5.   Seek the advice of a local expert

For successful flipping, a real estate agent would be of great help because he will help you identify the right properties, offer advice on the kind of renovations that could lift the face of the property, and help you sell quickly.

Rent, Interest, Tax Benefits, and Appreciation

Regardless of the kind of property you own, the benefits you reap from your ownership of real estate property are in the following forms:

Rent

Rent refers to all forms of payment made to the owner of a townhome, single-family home, commercial building, condo, industrial and crowd-funded real estate. Most people that choose to invest in real estate indicate a preference towards investing in property and leasing it all out to a tenant. Rental income is a source of stability because it is predictable, steady and consistent, especially in a market with a high population because a high demand leads to high rent rates.

Therefore, when you want to invest in property that could bring you income in the form of rent, ensure that you go through the list of local vacancy rates to determine the kind that is most needed by the customers.

Some property owners choose to pocket the entire amount they make through rent payments and then take up all duties that related to the upkeep and maintenance, but other property owners decide to take up the maintenance, upkeep and other services of a property management company in exchange for a small percentage of all rent paid. Drawing from the typical average rates, assume that a property manager will ask for 10% of the gross amount collected, for long-term renters. The commission rate for short-term rentals is much higher.

Interest

The returns that real estate investment companies and private equity firms pursue in their generation of real estate profits generation pursuit are called interest. The details of this method are simple: someone gives the real estate developer or investor a loan to buy property and then collect back the interests and the fees charged, and through this method, he can generate profits.

If you take up this strategy, you take on the role of the bank as the source of funding. This is a legitimate investing strategy for the real estate market.

Tax Benefits

One of the realities of the real estate market that many fail to notice are the tax benefits. When you invest in real estate, you are immediately turned into a nosiness owner, and in this capacity, you are entitled to tax deductions, in the United States at least. These deductions will cut through the costs you incur maintaining and upgrading your property, cleaning and maintenance supplies you purchase, traveling expenses and other costs you bear.

So far, however, depreciation is the most attractive thing about investing in real estate. Depression is the sack of gold coins at the end of the glistening rainbow that the investor collects at the end of each tax year. Simply, the IRS allows investment property owners to depreciate the value of their property over a specified period. To be specific, investors are allowed to devalue their properties every 27 and a half years.

Let's say that you purchase a property for $ 300,000. The IRS will allow a (300,000/27.5) tax loss every year, for 27.5 years, or for the length of time you will hold the property. If you do the math, that's a $10,909 tax loss each year.

There is a catch, however. Besides having to 'recapture' this amount when you sell, the $10k plus tax deduction per year outweighs having to pay back to the IRS a portion, later.

Appreciation

In some real estate markets where the costs of property keep moving up-wards, owners of property can earn returns only for purchasing and holding the property. This increase in value is called appreciation, and it translates into profits one the property is sold.

This investment method is suitable for people looking to invest in the long-term particularly in a market where prices are forever moving upwards. Investors in this market should be comfortable with just the long-term-buy-and-hold strategy because even without having to develop the property or do anything else similar to that, the prices are guaranteed to rise and the property will have appreciated.

Are You Suited for Real Estate Investing?

Investing in real estate is trendy, and everyone will want to get in a piece of the action seeing that the value of real estate will most certainly rise. Everyone likes to outsmart the system and make some extra cash. However, the reality is that real estate is not a trade for everyone. Some people will excel at it while others are better off pursuing alternative investment options.

If you want to assess whether real estate is the right investment vehicle for you, consider the following factors:

Do you possess the skills needed for investing in real estate?

Unlike other forms of investment, real estate investing requires that you can make careful considerations, calculation, and monitoring to excel and to keep tabs of the market landscape. If you are going to outsource the services of a property manager, you need to come up with a plan detailing how you are going to deal with them. If you choose to maintain your property yourself, you need to plan on how you will handle the upkeep and maintenance work, and this can be challenging and time-consuming.

Think about the tenants. Some tenants are problematic: some won't pay rent; some will make it unbearable for other tenants while others could damage your property. Ask yourself whether you are able or are ready to handle this before earlier on.

Lastly, ensure that you are motivated, you have adequate knowledge of the market, and that your organizational skills are on point before you make an investment decision.

Market Favorability

Even when you have the right skills, the knowledge and the capital you would need to start investing in real estate, making a move as at now would be wrong. For example, if you are operating in a market that is on a declining trend, on top of a bull market, it will be difficult or impossible for you to profit from investing in real estate.

That is not to say, however, that any time the market is in an unfavorable position you should shy away from making investments. Even in times like these, you can still invest by looking for investment opportunities outside your area and favoring those that are in a much better market climate.

Adequacy of Resources

You should never invest by paying a down payment of money you would not be comfortable losing. Therefore, avoid going all in on investment property if losing the money you have invested would leave you in a dire financial situation were it to fail.

The Commitment

If you intend to lease or rent your property, be ready for the responsibilities and the demands that come with owning property like that. For example, you will need to coordinate cleaning, emptying trash cans, collect rent, conduct repairs, screen the tenants, and various other tasks that you cannot afford to fail.

Note that if you do not have the time or the ability to do any of these things, you have the option of paying someone to assist you in doing it, but this will dig through your income a bit.

Chapter 2: The Benefits of Real Estate to Help You Reach Financial Freedom

There is a lot of freedom and flexibility when it comes to working in real estate. You get the benefit of working hours that fit with your schedule. If you are willing to be patient and look around the market for some time, you will find properties that can make you a lot of money each month. And there are so many options when it comes to real estate that it won't take long before you find the avenue that is the best one for you.

Many people get into real estate each year. And they have big dreams of making it big and seeing some great profits. And those who are willing to put in the work and not give up because of a few minor road blocks along the way will see this profit. That is the amazing thing about real estate. There are always people looking to purchase a home or rent a home or apartment to live in, and you can profit off that if you are willing to search your area, learn about the market and what rental rates are, and are willing to put in the hard work.

There is going to be hard work. You won't become rich off your first property. If you get that property for a good price, and you can keep the refurbishment costs down, you may be able to bring home some profits each month fairly quickly. But if you really want to grow your rental property business, you won't use that money for personal reasons yet. You will reinvest it into another property, and then another one, and then another one.

Before you know it, you have ten, twenty, thirty, or more properties that you own, and people paying you each month to live in them! Add in your own property manager who can take care of the day-to-day running of those properties (so that you don't have to), and you will see how rental properties can become a passive form of income. Think about how much financial freedom this can give you!

Of course, this is going to be a method that takes some work on your part. You aren't going to be able to just purchase one or two properties that are in perfect condition for a good price and then make a lot of money in the process. But if you are willing to put in some of the hard work, you will be able to walk away with a good income each month. And if you plan it all right, get the right properties, and find a good property manager, you are going to be able to make a lot of money on these without having to do a lot of work on your own over time.

There are a lot of benefits that come with working with real estate and choosing that as your way of earning an income and gaining financial freedom. Some of these include:

• You get to make the decisions: When you decide that it is time to invest in an income property, you are the one who gets to make the decisions. You can choose the property that you want to invest in, whom you will rent to (as long as you meet the local laws in your area), how much you are going to charge for the rent, and how you would like to manage and maintain the property.

• Property appreciation: With rental properties, you get to purchase the property with just a bit of your own money. You then borrow the rest from a lender. This is known as leverage and is going to help you earn more. Even if you only rent out the property for ten years, the price of the home will go up, even though the amount you owe overall to the bank will go down, and you can take a bigger profit in the end.

• Rental income is real money that you get to keep. If you plan to place tenants in the investment property, then you will receive a real income each month. After you pay off the mortgage and any other debts or maintenance that you have on the property, you get to pocket the rest of the rent! The better the price you get the property for, the more money you will make each month.

- Tenants are going to pay down the mortgage for you. And the longer you hold onto the property, the more of the loan principal your tenant is going to end up paying. You will take your rental money each month and put it towards paying off that loan, rather than using your own money!

- Lots of tax write-offs. When you own a rental property, there are a lot of great tax deductions that you get to work with including property taxes, professional and legal fees, travel expenses, maintenance repairs, insurance, an interest that you pay on the credit cards to fix up the property, and mortgage interest. You can also count the depreciation of the purchase price of the property, even when the property is appreciating in value.

When it comes to helping your business grow and succeed, and when you want to make sure that you actually reach the financial freedom that you are looking for, then working with rental properties is the best option for you.

Chapter 3: How to Read the Market

No matter if you are choosing to get into rental properties or into flipping homes, it is important that you have a good idea on how to read the market. This will help you to know when property values are low, and when they are higher, so that you can purchase and sell them at the right time to maximize your profits. If you aren't willing to learn about the market, and understand how it works, then you are likely to purchase too high and sell too low, and your profits will either be low, or nonexistent.

In this chapter, we are going to take a look at how you can read the market cycle of real estate. While this isn't going to be an exact science, and no guarantee knowing this information is going to always get you the best prices, it is one of the best ways to understand when to buy and sell to get the best profits. So, let's dive in and learn more about how to read this cycle.

Understanding the Real Estate Market

Before we go too far into some of the specifics on the market and how to analyze and predict it, we need to make sure that we understand, and are on the same page, when it comes to the term real estate market. This is basically just a phrase that is used in order to describe the economic state of real estate, whether in the country as a whole or just in one area or market. This is often going to be based on the supply and demand for properties in that area.

This thought on the real estate market is actually pretty broad, and it doesn't go into some of the more complicated parts of this market at all. When we are going to talk about some of the conditions of the economy in general with real estate, the details are going to be the part that is the most important. For example, you may want to consider some of the following thoughts when you hear about the real estate market, and tell if they are different or the same from one another:

•   Are we talking about the real estate market and how it is doing in one specific location? The market for California could be widely different than what you are going to see in Iowa for example.

•   Are you looking at the real estate market and trying to see how it does in a specific niche? This could include things like hotels, office buildings, apartments or single-family homes. It is possible that at this point in time it is great to purchase a single-family home, but finding a good deal on an apartment complex may be out of the questions.

•   Are you talking about the market for real estate for a certain user? The market may be quite a bit different for someone who wants to rent compared to someone who wants to purchase. A buyer may find that the market is great because there are a lot of properties on the market to choose from, but the seller has a lot of competition and may think that the market is bad.

No matter which of these you are talking about, the real estate market that we talked about above is going to be based on the demand and supply of real estate, regardless of what the user thinks, what the niche is, or even the location. Even so, and even with all of these changes, there are going to be some patterns that you are able to analyze, which will help you out with your investment.

The Four Phases of The Real Estate Cycle

One thing that you may find interesting when you first get into real estate is that the whole process is going to be cyclical. What this means is that there will be a lot of repetition that you can watch out for. And if you miss one of the phases in the cycle, just hold on because it is going to come back around for you again. The cycle is not going to be steady and it always moves at its own pace. Sometimes it will go quickly and sometimes it will go slowly. And a single market may see that their cycle is going in a different speed or direction that you would find when you look at the national market as a whole.

There are four main phases of the real estate market, and once the four are done, the market will go back and start it all over again. These four phases are going to be known as:

1. Recovery

2. Expansion

3. Hyper supply

4. Recession

First off is phase one of recovery. During this phase, the real estate cycle, which really doesn't have a beginning and can start anywhere in the four phases, we are just starting here to make it easier, the market is going to be recovering from the downturn that is going to show up at times in the cycle. This is a time when the market is not in free fall that it was before, and it is starting to go through an upward trend.

For a home buyer and an investor alike, this is going to be a great time to purchase some real estate because it is often the bottom of the cycle, or when the properties are going to be at their lowest. If you wait too long after this time, then the market will go back up and the property values will go up as well.

This phase of the cycle is going to be represented by a high level (even though it is starting to stabilize) unemployment, a high number of home foreclosures, and a lot of fear that the general population will have about the economy as a whole. This may be the time when you hear other people say that it is a bad thing to invest in real estate because they know so and so lost a lot of money when doing it.

Then there is the second phase, which is the phase of expansion. This is the place where businesses in that area are starting to add in more employees to their ranks, and you will see that many people are starting to feel more confident in real estate again, which is making it grow.

This is the phase where you are going to see the prices of homes start to rise quite a bit, and it is going to be triggered by a decrease in the supply of available properties, but a climbing amount of demand. There are more and more people during this phase who are looking to purchase properties because they think that it is more of an advantage than living with their family or renting the property.

It is possible that during this phase, a lot of businesses are going to decide to expand as well, which cuts down on the available commercial buildings. Thanks to this expansion, developers in real estate are going to start building up new homes, as well as some new properties, to try and cater to this demand.

When you are in this phase of the cycle, you know that it is the perfect time to start investing in real estate. The rising prices of rents can help you make more, while the prices of the properties are still pretty low. And a lot of people have a general outlook on the market that is optimistic. If you act early enough in this phase, you will still be able to find some good deals because the market is dealing with a bit of a mess from the foreclosures that were there before. You will have to put in a bit more work here to get them.

This is a great market to be a part of, but you need to act quickly and be on the lookout. It is possible that even during this period of growth, there are some big problems in the guise of speculators that will enter the picture. These speculators are a type of investor who is going to rely very heavily on the amount of growth that happens in this market to help them generate profits. And they are going to make sure that their numbers are based on this need.

Do not become a speculator. Many times, these investors are not playing it smart and they are going to pay way more for an investment property than they should, simply because they can. This can lead to the next phase, and homes that are way overpriced for the market.

Now we move into what is known as the third phase of the market cycle, which is going to be a boom cycle of hyper supply. If you were someone who paid a lot of attention to the real estate market in America during the mid-2000s, you would see that this era was one that had a lot of prices that skyrocketed, mass building projects, and everyone you talked to wanted to purchase and invest in real estate because they thought they would become rich overnight.

This kind of hyper supply is going to be caused, at least in large part, by a lot of builders who are willing to pay more for the land and any construction than they should. They are doing this because they are basing their numbers on the idea that the price they can set for rents will rise indefinitely, and this will justify what they are paying. House flippers who aren't careful could end up doing the same thing, and this causes them to pay too much for the property, simply because they know that there is another person who will come out and overpay for the work that they did.

You will notice that the demand is going to start leveling off a bit during this time as the supply that was built before will reach more of an equilibrium. This means that during the expansion phase, new construction is going to be built to accommodate the increased demand for real estate, and at some point, it is going to catch up, and the amount of supply will equal the demand.

Now, if we were living in a perfect world, there would be some stabilization in the market and everyone would be happy. But because real estate development is going to be a slow process, and can take a few years, the construction that some people started during the last phase will continue at big speeds. The supply is going to overtake the demand, and there will be a rise in the vacancies. The house of cards that come here will be the greater fool theory, and it is primed for that wind, or the market cycle, to come and knock it over.

When you are in this period of the market, there can be a lot of stories about wealth and how much people have been able to make in real estate, will come out. And these are not all lies because some people who got in early and made smart decisions were actually making money. But at some point, the costs will get too high, and the demand will go down, and it will stop. And way too many people, who jumped in without thinking through the process and how much longer it would last, will end up losing.

To avoid coming into the market during this time, when the costs are high and there aren't any profits to be made, to really crunch the numbers. There are going to be a lot of stories out there about how much money you are able to make. But if you crunch the numbers and it isn't adding up, then it is time to step back and wait the market to cycle out.

And now it is time to work on the final phase, the recession. In this phase, you can look at some of the building projects, the ones that were promising a few years before, can't be sold, which will drive down the prices fast. The foreclosures are going to go high like crazy, and many owners are going to be underwater. Investors are going to find that it is difficult to pay their mortgage because they have to decrease the rents they charge, or because they have more vacancies as people can't afford to rent either.

In some cases, this recession in real estate can happen along with a recession in the economy, like what was seen in 2007 and 2008, and it is easy to see why millions of homeowners were out of work, not able to pay their mortgages on time, and we're finding out that they paid too much for the property to start with.

This is maybe a bad time for those investors who are already in the market and who purchased the property at a price that was way too high, but it is perfect for new investors who are willing to get into the market and hold onto the property for some time. While everyone else is worried and upset that they paid much for the properties, the smart investors are waiting it out for the bottom so that the supply will once again dip below the demand where a great deal can be found.

Once the market does get to this bottom, this is the best time for an investor to get in and find some of the best deals possible, and help out other homeowners in the process. While other people may be running away from real estate during this time, a smart investor will see that the market is bottoming out, and that, since it is a cycle, it will go back up soon. They will take up properties at a great rate, and then rent them out and wait it all out until the economy goes back up again, and the market enters into the expansion or the hyper-supply again, where they are able to make a huge profit in the process.

After looking at these four parts of the market cycle, it is time to analyze where you are currently, especially in the market where you would like to buy and sell. If you notice that it is in a recession, then it is time to hold onto your property and wait for things to go up. But it is the perfect time to purchase a property because you will be able to get it for a good price. The recovery is another place to purchase for the same thing.

The expansion phase can work as well if you are careful and crunch the numbers. But you need to be careful. But once the phase of hyper supply comes in, it is time to sell if you are flipping the home and stay out of the market if you are looking to purchase. The prices are way too high, and things are going to start going back here soon, which can cut you out of the profits in no time.

The best way to look at how the market cycle is doing in your area, and whether or not it is a good time to purchase or sell is the supply and demand. If you look around your market and notice that there are a lot of properties for sale, and they have been on the market for more than a few weeks, then you are probably in a recession or a recovery and the prices are going to be lower because of the competition.

However, if you notice that the properties are going fast, and that the prices are really high, you may be in an expansion, or the hyper supply. This would be a good time to sell a property because you can get a really high price on it. But it would be a horrible time to purchase because you will end up spending way too much and would have a hard time actually being able to sell for high enough to make a profit.

As you can see, having a good idea of how the market cycle works, and where you are currently in that market cycle will influence whether you are purchasing or selling properties. Being able to read and understand this market is the best way to ensure that you are actually able to make a profit through all of this.

Chapter 4: The Different Types of Real Estate Properties

Real estate is possibly the most popular and the oldest of the investment classes. Although many people know that, not many understand the different types of real investment properties, which limits their investment ability, portfolio, and even basic interest. Of course, each of them has its own risks and benefits as you shall see.

Here are some of the real estate property types:

Turnkey Property

The word 'turnkey' is coined from the idea that the real estate property has been made ready for occupation and all that the investor needs to do after purchase is to 'turn the key.' Underneath this loose definition, what exactly is a turnkey property?

A turnkey real estate property is an apartment building or home that has been renovated, and an investor can immediately purchase and live in or rent out. This kind of property is traditionally purchased from companies that specialize in the renovation of an old property. Fortunately, these same companies offer property management services to their customer, which significantly reduces the amount of effort and time that the investors have to spend on the property they have purchased.

Turnkey properties became popular during the 2007–2008 recession that came after the housing bubble burst. At the time, buying and owning a home became cheaper than renting in many parts of the country. This investment approach did and still does attract, people who want to be involved in the real estate business but lack the ability or tie to handle the renovation and maintenance issues of a home. In many cases, the investors have hired an independent company to handle the property management processes, but with time, there has emerged real estate companies that offer a complete package, including the maintenance.

How Turnkey Properties Generate Income

Once an investor has purchased a turnkey property, it is expected that it will be available for occupation immediately because the idea behind acquiring real estate that needs little to no refurbishment is to ensure that the property starts to generate revenue immediately. The only work that may remain includes plumbing repairs, replacing electrical fixtures, flooring fixes where necessary and adding a fresh coat of paint to the interior. With only these few changes to make, the sooner the property is ready for rent, the faster the returns on investment will start flowing in.

It does not make sense to renovate a home fully if the intention is to sell it rather than putting it for rent. The expenses that a developer will put into conducting the repairs such as adding a new coat of paint may not be the selling point that buyers are looking for because each comes with his or her own ideas about how the place should look like. This also means that the real estate agent should not be involved in the tearing down or doing away with any refurbishment that the current owner did. After all, the money the agent will spend on the repairs is only likely to increase the asking price of the property. Therefore, the only repairs you should be conducting are only those that will bring the building up to code.

Benefits of Turnkey Properties

The most obvious of the benefits is the fact that there are more properties to consider when buying. If you took the time to study the area in which you live, you would be able to assess the houses that are for sale. Where the number is large, the prices will be low, which means that you can save some significant amount if you have this information beforehand.

Second, turnkey properties are a great source of passive income, which is the entire reason people invest. Owning and being in charge of the management of a property is a full-time job, and purchasing a turnkey property gives you the freedom to step away from all the heavy lifting, and you only focus on ensuring that the property is giving you back your investment. Your earnings should go upwards gradually, only demanding little, if any, effort from you. If you go further and employ a property manager, then you no longer have to care for the property, you only have to wait for the returns.

Third, buying a turnkey property implies that you are buying the specific property for less, which makes the property a better deal, especially because of the income you expect to make from it. If you contract the services of a turnkey real estate company, the company will go ahead and buy the property and clean it up before presenting it to you. Once the sale is complete, leave the property with them. Although they will make money from managing the property, you will be the legal owner.

(A turnkey real estate company is similar in form to a regular real estate company, only that they deal primarily with turnkey investors. They use their expertise and experience to offer investment advice to their customers.)

Risks Behind Turnkey Investing

The risks include:

a) It is risky to entrust your investment to another to manage it.

Although turnkey properties are preferred because the investor does not have to spend too much time on it, this kind of arrangement can be quite risky. You will be leaving the responsibility of assessing the tenants and renting to a company. Giving away your freedom of choice and decision-making can be difficult to do. Therefore, ensure that you scout the market for the best property management company, and then take your hands off, allowing them to take charge from there.

b) The possibility of lacking tenants

Once it is newly released to the market, the property may not have some or all tenants for a while. This is the reason why many turnkey investors advocate for owning more than one house so that when some units are empty, the buildings with more occupied units may support the others. If you only own one house and do not get tenants to occupy it for a while, you will have to bear the burden of absorbing the cost of management and the probable loan you have.

c) The risk of buying unseen

This mainly happens when investors buy property through real estate companies without really seeing it before the refurbishing and assessing its potential. This is risky because it could work both for and against you because you could end up purchasing some property that costs more in terms of maintenance, nibbling away a considerable amount of the profits.

From the assessment, turnkey properties are not ideal for all people. However, if you want to invest in a considerably expensive area, then the turnkey strategy is the way to go because you will use less money than you would be buying the land and then constructing it. It is an ideal investment vehicle for investors that want to invest and gain that extra passive income without having to go over the management process. Therefore, depending on how involved you want to be, choose the proper way to invest in turnkey properties.

Vacation Rental

A vacation rental is a property that is purchased to be used as a second home or a rental property that brings in income to offset the costs of maintenance and to bring a profit. Vacation rental property is best purchased in an area that is popular as a vacation destination so that the property can be rented often.

Ensure that you invest in a location that is frequented by tourists, one that has attractions like casinos, beaches, national parks, lakes or mountains. The place should have adequate and high standard amenities. Recently, vacation rental properties have become a popular alternative for tourists looking for alternative accommodation while on vacation. Most tourists now prefer the home setup instead of living in a hotel and will opt to rent a house for as long as their vacation will last.

Investors can find vacation rentals advertised online, from a turnkey real estate company or with the help of realtor working locally at the vacation destination. Your choice of real estate property should be guided by the popularity of the destination you have chosen, the expected returns on investment, the affordability of the property, the rental market rates in the short-term and the occupancy rate of the hotels and vacation rental properties around. Therefore, in your search, opt for a tourist area that not only has the main attractions in the area but also has an investment advantage.

For example, Las Vegas is famous for its casinos, Orlando is known for Disneyworld, Pensacola is popular due to its location on the coast while Nashville attracts tourists for its music scene. While these cities have some of the best attractions, some like San Francisco and New York are said to be too expensive, and the returns on investment are not adequate.

Always target areas whose local occupancy rates reach 70% and above. This makes an excellent rule of thumb that is useful for when you are deciding on the location to make your investment. You must keep in mind the fact that many of the tourist destinations are seasonal which means that the occupancy rate, among other indicators, will fluctuate.

Rent rates also change in the short-term. Ask yourself if you can afford to pay all your bills even when the tenants are yet to arrive or when the rents fluctuate depending on the tourism season. If you can cover the bills comfortably, you can go ahead and invest in a vacation rental.

You should also consider looking for a vacation rental that makes sense financially. Perform a cost-benefit analysis to ensure that you can afford the apartment even when its occupancy is zero. Consider the vacancy rates of other similar businesses in the area as well as their short-term rates, and compare them to your costs of operation and monthly financing.

Ways to Make Money with Vacation Rental Properties

The most popular ways of making money with this kind of property include renting it out as an Airbnb, VRBQ and for hosting hotel programs.

Airbnb

Airbnb is an online application that allows property owners to rent their vacation property to tourists who are looking for hotel room alternatives. To market the property as an Airbnb, you need to create a profit using a description of the amenities that the guests stand to enjoy. The charges that require payment from you include a 3–5% service charge for every booking. If taxes are relevant to your situation, they should also be added. All costs are then subtracted out of the host's payout.

Hotel Program

This is another money-making option for owners of property like this. Hotel programs are for locations that are already enrolled in a hotel plan such that the investor is allowed to take up the hotel's management services to manage the hotel program by himself. This option is suitable for people who want to rent to their property but want to do it under a strict rental schedule. The rates for these rentals are higher than those of Airbnb because of the hotel services offered.

VRBO

The Vacation Rental by Owner is an online branded site where vacation owners advertise their property for tourists visiting the area can see it. Investors manage the property themselves or hire a property manager to take care of business, including that of marketing the site online. This kind of rental is different from the Airbnb because of its different fee structures.

For example, the property owner has to pay $399 as an annual fee for when using long-term rentals, and an 8% booking fee, which is interchangeable with a 13% booking fee if you want the company to manage the property for you. These costs are subtracted automatically from the investor's payout.

Multifamily Home

Investing in a multifamily home that contains two or more units is different from investing in a single family home. You probably will need to take up a loan to facilitate the purchase.

Below are six factors to consider when researching the structure of the neighborhood, and when choosing the lender, in a process that should not take longer than 2 to 3 weeks.

1. Research neighborhoods that would make excellent investment grounds.

You need to decide on a suitable neighborhood even though you will not be living there. Your property should be at a location that is desirable to tenants, so that the units may be occupied as soon as possible. You could first look into the neighborhoods that have multifamily homes up for sale before narrowing down to your home of choice.

In your search, take note of the following factors: the attractions, the amenities, the walk score, rating of schools there, availability of public parking, availability of public transportation, the businesses nearby, the condition of properties around and the overall condition of the area. Conduct this research with the help of a local real estate agent, and then drive around the city to see these things for yourself.

A good rule is to choose a property that is utmost an hour to your desired property's location from where you live because it makes it easier to drive there to meet contractors, inspect the property, and make service calls.

2. Find a lender and get pre-approved.

Once you have found your choice property, get a lender who offers multi-family loans and whose application process is easy. The lender will give you a pre-approval letter which you can submit to the seller to make your offer. Lenders are best sourced online because getting a local lender who specializes in multifamily homes can be quite a task. Check the lender's rates, terms, customer service, areas it covers, and the conditions of the property that it can cover. Your local real estate agent, the bank, or even another investor may also be able to refer you to a lender.

Your choice lender will seek some introductory financial information which is meant to get you pre-approved or pre-qualified. He will then give you a pre-approval letter indicating how much money you qualify for and the interest rates for that amount. The letter will signal to sellers that you are serious and will afford to purchase the property.

The letter should act as a guide for your budget because that may be the only money you get for investment. Factor in the costs you are likely to incur such as the renovation costs, repair costs, carrying costs (insurance, taxes, utilities, mortgage), and the closing costs (title insurance, lender fees, property taxes, and property insurance).

3. Seek an agent's services.

Although you may have laid out facts on the table already, your budget and possible neighborhoods to invest in, you still need to work with a real estate agent, especially one who is knowledgeable about multifamily properties and one who has worked in that neighborhood a while. An agent will help refine the search, arrange for showings and help you negotiate a price.

Choose an agent based on his or her availability, experience (of at least two years) with multifamily properties, location, and specialty.

4. Narrow down the search to a single property.

Once you have thoroughly researched neighborhoods, your pre-approval letter in hand, and an excellent agent by your side, it is time to narrow down the search to the single property you want to purchase. Although your budget and choice of a neighborhood should have already narrowed down the search, it is also important to ensure that the property will have a positive cash-flow now and in the days to come. Also check the condition of the property, the rent roll, the vacancy rate and the expected revenue versus expected expenses to see if it makes sense to invest in that property.

5. Boldly make an offer.

Once you have found the ideal property, make an offer. From this point, the real estate agent carries the load, and to this point, you need some clean deposit money to accompany your pre-approval letter. The offer you make should be subject to your financing and appraisal. This means that if your loan is not approved even after an honest application, you will not lose your deposit. It also means that the property ought to appraise the sales price agreed upon, or you will not make the purchase.

A multifamily property must have more contingencies than would a single-family property because you will need time to conduct your due diligence about the rental history of the property. The due diligence takes about 15 days, and the owners should be able to provide you with the rent roll, costs of maintenance, tenant payment history, and others. Examine these details to help you make a final decision on whether you still want to pursue that offer.

6. Receive the funding and close on the deal.

After making an offer and presented your pre-approval letter, it is time to get the actual funding. This is where your lender gives you a financing commitment. The commitment is stronger than the approval letter because by now, the lender has had more time to look into your details and confirmed the information you provided.

For funding, you will need to provide additional details like the property appraisal, a complete mortgage application, documentation showing the source of the deposit amount, purchase contract, details of the property, rent roll and lease copies, and the application fee if they asked for it. Before you go to the closing, ensure that you get insurance for the property and landlord insurance for yourself.

At the closing, the seller and yourself will sign some documents. The seller will transfer all the security deposits paid to you, and you will receive the keys to your new property.

Apartment Rental

Many people dream of collecting rental income from owning an apartment or a number of them. This idea is especially attractive because, in many cities of the world, rental houses are in short supply while the demand is high, driving the costs up high, all the while, allowing the property owner to reap the benefits. The demand for rental houses is not about to go down because more people want to live closer to where they work, which means that people who own property near downtown or property that has an ease of commute into the workplaces stand to benefit from the attractiveness of their property to the growing workforce, year after year.

Property owners who do not have time to be landlords can hire property management companies to take on this responsibility. The company does this at a cost, which means that the investor has to weigh out the costs of handing over the property management role versus the time and energy he is willing to dedicate to the new business.

If all of the above mentioned has picked your interest, look out for the pros and cons discussed below:

Benefits

- Apartment buildings are easier to scale.

In only one purchase, you get to own multiple housing units, all under the same roof. One transaction could get you to hold 5, 20 or even 100 units. The high number of units might make management somewhat challenging, but the returns are high too. What's impressive is that it will take you an equal amount of time to acquire so many units, as opposed to building a unit at a time.

- Easier to finance

A real estate owner who owns more than five units owns a commercial building, and this makes him eligible for a business loan. Loans like these are easier to obtain compared to residential loans because they are based on investment rather than person liabilities and assets.

- The benefit of economies of scale

The fact that all your investment is under one roof makes maintenance easier and cheaper. If you have a leaking roof, you only have to replace one roof as opposed to what you would do it you owned ten single-family houses, and they all had leaking roofs. You also only need one insurance plan, and you will need the services of one property management firm. Everything is done once, and for the benefit of all housing units.

- Gives you more control over the value

The value of a building is tied to its performance and the revenue the owner receives from it through the collection of rent. Therefore, repositioning the building in an intelligent and savvy way will lead you to enjoy more benefits and in a quick way.

Risks

- Requires intensive management

Typically, property owners experience issues and difficulties when dealing with tenants. Therefore, with a larger number of them living in your apartment rental building, expect that a more significant amount of issues will arise.

Other unforeseen issues arise, which could impact the amount of money you receive as rental income. For example, a tenant could lose his job and not be able to pay rent for some months or a family could split and the partner that remains might not be able to cover the rent by himself. There is also the issue of children who in their adventures come up with a million ways to destroy your property.

Generally, accommodating a community of people in your property is a lot of work.

- The costs increase.

The larger the number of units to be maintained, the higher the costs of maintenance. Think about it: the costs of disposing garbage will increase driven by the frequency and the amount to be disposed of, the water bill will rise, and the amount you have to pay to the property management company will be higher than if you were paying for the maintenance of a single unit.

- Your attention is still required.

You need to know that even if you hire a property manager, your attention and time will still be required to an extent.

- Cannot be moved quickly in the market

In addition, unlike stocks that you can sell readily, this is not the case for an apartment building, and if you do, you will lose handsomely.

- Requires a lot of reserve money

You will need to keep aside a lot of money to cover the repairs and the unexpected vacancies too. Keep in mind that many of the monthly expenses are fixed and do not depend on the occupancy rate. Therefore, these bills have to be paid whether the units are all occupied or not.

Commercial Rental

Commercial real estate is the kind that is leased out specifically for retail and business purposes. Common categories include space for offices, hospitals, retail, industrial, leisure, and even some multi-family housing. Land that has been purchased with the intention of erecting any of the spaces mentioned is also classified under the commercial property category.

It is an undeniable fact that commercial real estate investing is one of the prime gateways towards building incredible passive wealth. This kind of investing has so many advantages over property bought for residential purposes, such as the potential to bring forth a higher income. The cash flow is steadier, leasing contracts made are more attractive, and the risks of vacancies are significantly lower.

However, commercial rentals are not without their own hurdles. These properties require potential investors to conduct due diligence before entering into a purchasing deal. One of the principal requirements is that the investor should research to study how commercial rentals work carefully.

Commercial rentals work this way: an investor purchases a property that is used only for business purposes, then leases the space he has bought to as many business units as the spaces available, and then collects rent from each of them. The businesses could be used for industrial, office, retail, warehousing, and other uses.

The Benefits of Commercial Rental

Investing in this kind of real estate can be rewarding, both financially and personally. Many do it to gain financial security and freedom in the days to come. Others take advantages of the tax benefits the property brings, and the increased diversity in their portfolios that the property brings.

Other advantages include:

Increased cash flow: One distinct advantage of commercial real estate is the ability to bring a consistent stream of income. Typically, commercial properties involve longer leases unlike the residential kind, which means that the rental income is reliable and steady.

In some cases, the tenants are also expected to pay the operating expenses of the commercial property in what is known as a triple net lease. This includes paying the building's insurance, maintenance cost, and taxes besides the monthly rent. This exempts the owner from these payments and increases the profit margin, hence, higher profits.

A higher income: The primary drive behind investing in commercial rentals is the high-income potential of the property. Generally speaking, commercial buildings offer higher returns on investment of about 6 to 12 percent while the single-family properties fetch 1 to 4 percent only.

In addition, the vacancy risk for commercial real estate is lower because the property is spread across different units, and lease agreements cover a longer time than those of residential property.

The competition is minimal: There is less competition in this investment venture because investing in building offices, malls, shopping complexes, and others are outside many investors' comfort zones. Very few are willing to take that risk.

Longer leases: One of the most attractive aspects of commercial real estate is the attractive lease contracts. Commercial buildings have leases that last long periods compared to residential buildings. Most tenants lease properties for many years.

Chapter 5: How to Turn Real Estate into a Long-Term Business

Name some of the wealthiest people you know or have heard of, and I bet you that 80% of your number, if not more than that, have made their wealth through real estate. These investors didn't start by owning many properties. They started small, with only one—and their businesses grew, taking on a third, a fourth, and so on. Many people say that real estate is one of the most significant vehicles to financial freedom, and indeed, the numbers are a confirmation.

Owning real estate property is not just a great way to build your long-term wealth—it is also one of the best ways to diversify your portfolio. The primary reason that human beings build long-term wealth and diversify their investments is to have something to lean on in their old age or something to fall back to when one type of business is not doing well or when it collapses.

When you want to go ahead and make a step towards investing, start by answering the following critical questions:

1.   What do you find more exciting and more fulfilling than residential and commercial real estate?

2.   How much money do you have for investing at your disposal?

3.   Are you looking to make the investments using your own money, or will you use other people's money? In case you opt to seek investors, is debt investing the way to go, or will you give them a share of your business?

4.   Is the investment or the business you are trying to build intended to be a part-time hobby, or are you looking to make it a full-time business? Could it also be a part-time interest that you hope will morph into a long-term business?

The above questions are essential to help you determine where you are headed with your investment efforts. The third question is particularly crucial because debt is what will ensure your speed in business. With a vast capital resource, you will be able to grab opportunities as they come and to make substantial investments that attract consumers more than the small investments, among other things. Money makes the entire investment process easier, more efficient, and therefore, more successful.

Once you have answered each of the questions above, you can now move on and begin your ascent following the steps and the advice below:

1. Embrace the Humble Start

If you haven't made any real estate investments in the past, do not jump ship with all your valuables. Avoid using all the resources you have—even if you can afford to do so. Not one of the successful real estate investors will tell you about how the first investment they made propelled them to greatness. You are still green in the business, and you need to learn the ropes of it. For example, you are yet to know how to read and interpret contracts—you still haven't built your network of real estate professionals, and you are yet to develop a right eye for the business. All this knowledge comes from experience and not from a textbook.

The beauty of the business is that you will have the opportunity to learn all the knowledge you would need just by the small deals. For example, you could try finding cheap properties—say, a single-family home, multi-units, or a commercial property—and use them to practice the trade by presenting them to customers and negotiating with them. Ensure that for the first several deals, you only commit very little as you get to learn the ropes of the trade.

If you do not have money to start buying property, do not let that slow you down—you can still do wholesaling. Wholesaling allows you to enter into a contract for a particular property, putting only very little money down, even less than $1000. You should then work hard to move the property before the contract expires. Best-case scenario, you will make between 5 and 15 grand that you can reinvest in other long-term holdings. Worst-case scenario, say you did not put any contingencies; you will only have lost a grand.

2. Go Big

The real estate business can be overwhelming sometimes, and it is easy to give up especially when you haven't got any money. However, the money ought not to scare you, the deals that you get into are the ones that matter. Therefore, as you turn your interest into a long-term business, ensure that you are pursuing the deal and not the money.

Someone was talking about a real estate investor who saved up $50,000 and then started chasing deals worth $200,000. The fact is that with that amount budgeted, you cannot pursue more than 4 units, and each of the units can only bring you $1,000 and $2,000 each month. What's more, you can only get this money after using thousands of dollars in renovations to make the units rentable. From this analysis, this money is just not enough.

For this reason, you must go big right from the start. Let's say that you take up a minimum of 16 units. Don't be tempted to take less than 16. Now, with 16 units, you can now take on the services of a manager, or you can now take the opportunity you now have to direct all your attention towards the property. Managing 16 units, you will need to wait and save some more money or pool other people's money. However, you will learn how to ask people for money, and you will learn how to sell.

3. Understand the Market, and Get a Mentor

In real estate, the choicest of the deals are the ones that are easiest to find like purchasing property that has management and a tenant in place. However, these properties will give you some of the lowest returns. However, the property and the deals that will provide you with the highest profits are those that other people do not know about, which you will find without any hustles.

For example, the best time to go about flipping houses is when the economy is strong, inventory levels are low, consumer confidence is high, and the interest rates are extremely low.

The low-interest rates allow the retail buyers to purchase a home rather than what they would have purchased when they are afraid of debt increasing under medium level and high-interest rates. The strong economy and high consumer confidence give the consumers the feeling that the right time to buy property is now. The low supply also called low inventory creates a high demand, which in turn causes investors to bid against each other, raising the property prices and allowing the investors to make more from the sale.

Therefore, if you can secure a property before the competition begins, then you will be able to transform your small initial investment into considerable returns in only a short period, particularly if you are flipping homes.

In case you are looking to make tax-advantaged passive income, the rise of the sharing economy through services like HomeAway and Airbnb have created short-term renting, which is no producing some of the highest returns on investment. You can even get 20% returns on good property that is located in areas with many attractions.

It is unfortunate, however, that there are still pitfalls in real estate. Therefore, you will need to educate yourself on some of the pitfalls that investors fall into, and how you can avoid them too. Source this knowledge from online sources but keep off the books, articles, and how-to videos because they contain little information especially in areas that investors should be wariest of. A mentor is also important because he will offer you advice based on the personal successes and failures he has had. He will also teach you some of the tricks he has acquired over the years, those that he uses to maneuver the market to get the best deals.

4. Prioritize Learning Against Earning

Yes, you have worked hard to earn that money, but before you spend it all on the 60-inch large curved smart TV you have been salivating over, consider spending that money educating yourself. Seminars and coaches are not a learning platform either. However, no matter how much they insist that you need an expensive education, you really do not. There is information everywhere, and the more substantial proportion of it is inexpensive; get it from someone who is an expert in real estate.

The way to grow your wealth in real estate is to build wealth by holding property. Having a shelter is one of the basic needs, which means that someone will come asking to rent your house for a specified period. As you purchase land in or around the metropolis areas, remember that land is a finite resource. If you cannot erect buildings at that particular time, someone else will. Therefore, if you own prime land, one of the immediate responses is to try and construct something. That rental will help you pay back the mortgage you took when purchasing your land. As you pay off your loan, choose to rent and to hold for something bigger,

In your investment, ensure that you do not spend beyond your budget. Most real estate projects you invest in will have surprises and overruns in them, but this is just the nature of the business. Therefore, keep aside some amount to cushion you against the unexpected. Levering your funds also help to lower risks and increase returns. What you do, you ought to start with one project, and then slowly graduate to the second. Continue making progress, and soon your real estate portfolio will be solid.

The most important lessons in real estate include the need to continually learn, hustle and aim for value addition or creation. Ensure that you take massive, ambitious courses of action every day. You also ought to speak to contractors and brokers every time you can; accompany them to meet-ups, or to view houses and on your way, learn something new. When you are ready to invest, knock the doors and ask to buy the property. The best deals are the ones where the owner is not prepared to sell. Find that property and then find someone to buy it, and you will have earned money on your first deal.

5. Make Your Mark Immediately

In real estate, there are three primary strategies you need to take note of:

The first is that you ought to purchase low-income property to start building your portfolio. Let's say you have bought a house for between $35,000 and $50,000. The costs of purchasing this property will be low, but you should expect consistent yields. On doing that, hand over the property to a property manager and start earning rental income passively. Assume that the returns will be of between 8% and 10%. Suppose you buy two or three more properties like this every year, in 10 years, you will have a portfolio of 20 or 3o houses, each giving you an amount I rental income. Already, you will have turned real estate into a long-term business.

The second strategy is that if you can do the repairs and fixing yourself, you ought to consider a 'live-in flip.' In this strategy, you begin by purchasing a house that only requires a little work on it for a great deal and lives on the property for about a year or two while you renovate the house. Once you are done, move out and flip the house for a higher value than you bought it, and you will earn a profit. Suppose you do this for five houses in 10 years, your earnings from these houses will fall in the $300,000 to $500,000 range net profits. This amount is enough to allow you to build or buy your own house or reinvest it into an apartment or commercial rentals that will cover your cost of living for the rest of your life.

The third strategy is to engage other people in a joint venture in a deal. Most people have the money or know where they can get it; they need some motivation and convincing that they are taking up the right opportunity. Therefore, to get them to give you the money, find an excellent deal and tie up that property with a contractual clause, pending finance approval for 30 days. In the meantime, find an investor to join forces with you in the flip. Explain to them that you have already secured the property on contract and that you only need the funds for a predetermined period, after which you will return the money and split the returns with him. So long as the deal looks reliable, you might be able to get almost anyone on board.

If only you make the right calls, you will easily find an investor with whom you can partner. Only ensure that you have correctly calculated the costs of the repairs and have estimated the expected sale price accurately. If you underestimate the costs of refurbishing the house and overestimate the price of the property in the market, the reality of things will chew into your returns, and you could lose credibility in the market.

6. The Returns Are in the Purchase

Many real estate investors think that the money lies in flipping which they commonly refer to as 'fixer-upper.' However, this is wrong because the money you pay for the property is what determines your profit margin once you sell. Therefore, the real money is in the purchase. Simply put, you make money when you buy the property, and not when you sell.

To ensure that you are buying right, compare the potential value of the property with that of three other similar sales, often called 'combs.' The combs that provide the best estimate are those of the same size, location and value as the property you are planning on purchasing.

That is not enough though; you need to ask yourself some critical questions. The first is, what would be the realistic sale price for the property after the rehabbing is complete? Secondly, in total, what is the scope of the work needed to attain this value? Do not allow your taste and preferences to cause you to push this value very high up.

Purchasing real estate property offers some core benefits such as it takes a short time to finish conducting the repairs and that the investor can reap some of the most significant profit margins while the cost of purchase is kept low and the price you paid to acquire the property is also very low.

However, before you actually embark on a project, ensure that you solidify both team A and team B. Team A is made up of experienced persons such as fellow investors, your mentor and your financial manager who will offer advice on the risks you can afford to take and those you should stay away from. Team B is made up of the associates who get you going including fellow investors, your mentor and your family.

Once you have built a solid plan, move along with your project. Avoid having backup plans because they keep you second-guessing yourself and prevent you from giving your best to what you are doing. However, ensure that you have many exit strategies to keep you from losing because even the most airtight plan may be flawed. Experienced investors say that real estate investment winds shift rapidly, and the worst thing you would want to have is to be stuck with a dozen unsellable properties.

Lastly, you ought to understand the difference between holding, buying, and trading. Buying you already know but this is no issue because the issue lies in what you do with what you have purchased. However, ensure that you hold on to commercial property for the long-term, but trade residential property as soon as you can.

7. Keep Time

For you to optimize the capital gains, you receive from your investment, and timing must be done properly. Real estate investors often use 12 p.m. and 6 p.m. metaphorically to indicate times that the market is at the peak and on the floor, respectively. Everyone wants to buy when the economy is doing well which pushes the prices upwards, but everyone sells when the market is at the bottom of the cycle.

The problem is that no one can accurately predict whether the market is resting precisely at 6 p.m. This makes the next best time to buy to be at 7 p.m. when the market starts moving up again slowly. Watch the market and coin your trend along the market trend so that you know when you buy and when you sell.

8. Your Intuition Matters

When you are investing in anything, not just for real estate investments do your homework in depth using all the analytics and the data you can find. Once you have done that, listen to your intuition, your gut feeling. Let both the data and your intuition lead you. Most investors say that some of the best deals they made were after careful consideration and carefully listening to their instincts.

Chapter 6: Real Estate Investment Options

There are many ways to make money in the real estate market, irrespective of what kind of property you choose to invest in. This chapter is dedicated to the various investment options you must make money in the real estate market.

Buy and Hold

The buy-and-hold strategy is what most novices in the real estate market start off with. In this option, you buy a piece of property, and hold it for the long term. Buying and holding it for the long term will be called so, irrespective of whether you purchase the real estate for monthly rents or for capital growth.

One of the primary reasons for the popularity of this investment strategy is that it is an accepted thing in the real estate market that the value of a property is more or less sure to double in about 7-10 years. Therefore, the buy-and-hold strategy is great for capital growth. However, while you are in possession of the home, you can also earn rental income from it.

So, summarily, the buy-and-hold investment option means you purchase a property, take the rental income as long as you choose to hold it, and then sell it for capital gains in the future.

Some buy-and-hold investors choose to take a rehabilitation loan to renovate the house which they were able to get at a cheap rate. This renovation will help in getting a better rent than before.

The buy-and-hold strategy is a perfect choice for passive real estate investors who are looking at owning the property for a long period of time to earn monthly rentals as a secondary and/or primary income. It is also a perfect strategy for people with multiple properties or landlords who are good at managing their real estate on their own. Here are some people who thrive in the real estate market using the buy-and-hold investment strategy:

Portfolio investors – These individuals own multiple (between 4-10) rental properties and use professional property management service providers.

Landlords – These people own up to 4 properties and are good at managing by themselves.

Turnkey properties – These people choose to buy rental properties in far-away places (away from where they live). Turnkey projects typically come with a tenant already in place, and the property is managed by professional companies.

1031 exchange – Many people buy property, hold it until the property value appreciates, then sell it at a higher price so that they can buy a bigger or better property. This approach helps such investors take advantage of the capital gains tax benefit referred to as 1031 exchange.

Costs associated with buy-and-hold strategies – Funding for the buy-and-hold strategy is generally done through the conventional mortgage route. The following expenses and costs are typical of most buy-and-hold investments:

- Costs of financing – loan origination fees, and other fees charged by the lender

- Closing costs – typically ranges between 25 and 5%

- Maintenance costs – towards maintenance and upkeep of the said property

- Utility payments – maintenance and upkeep of the common areas associated with the property

- Property taxes

- Insurance premiums

- HOA fees (if any)

Risks of the buy-and-hold strategy – The primary risks associated with this kind of investment strategy are low occupancy rates and potential depreciation of property prices. Low occupancy rates can be countered by pricing your rents to cover the vacancy periods.

Price depreciation may not directly be in your control. However, you can have control over this element too by researching and choosing properties in neighborhoods that have a potential for growth. Let us look at some of the risks connected with the buy-and-hold real estate investment strategy:

Occupancy risk – Rental properties are not always filled by tenants. They tend to remain vacant between tenants during which time you will not be earning any rent. Additionally, you could have tenants who maintain your property poorly resulting in reduced ROI as you will have to spend more money on repair and maintenance.

Price depreciation – It is possible for a property to lose value over time resulting in its price becoming less than the mortgage amount which means the investor owes more money than the worth of the property. This situation is referred to as 'the investor is underwater.'

Defaulting on the loan – Monthly amortization payments can sometimes become such a huge burden for buy-and-hold investors that they end up defaulting, and even becoming delinquent, on the payments. Such unfortunate situations can potentially lead to foreclosure or even bankruptcy, either of which can hurt your credibility significantly.

Personal defaults usually happen when an overenthusiastic investor borrows more money than he or she can pay back or when portfolio investors invest in more properties than they can handle at once. If you are prudent with your real estate investments, personal default can rarely occur.

Liability risk – Any on-site injuries caused by lack of or insufficient repair and maintenance or negligence can come to haunt portfolio investors and landlords. These investors invariably insure themselves with landlord liability insurance.

Fix and Flip

The fix-and-flip investment strategy is for short-term investors who can identify and pick up property that is in poor shape, fix it, and then sell it for a much higher price than the cost for profits. Typically, such investors want to complete the entire cycle of buying, fixing, and selling properties within a span of 12 months.

The fix-and-flip strategy is ideal for brokers, contractors, and realtors who have plenty of experience in the real estate market. Additionally, experienced rehabbers use this strategy to build wealth. Ideally, the fix-and-flip investment strategy is best for rehabbers who have some amount of experience in rehabilitation. However, in today's real estate markets, you can find professional rehabilitation agents who can take up the contract even for novice real estate investors.

Here are some useful tips on how to make the fix-and-flip strategy make money for you:

First, create a concrete flipping plan – You must have a clear, goal-oriented, and time-bound business plan to succeed in the fix-and-flip investment strategy. This plan not only gives you a clear pathway for progress with well-defined milestones, but it will also boost lender confidence in your capability and commitment in finishing the project successfully. Your flipping plan should have the following elements:

- Specific and time-bound goals including details of how you plan to achieve them

- Types of properties you plan to target along with reasons for your choice

- Location of the property

- Who is going to do the rehabilitation work? A paid contractor or you yourself? Reasons and separate plans have to be enclosed for this too

- Timeline of the entire project, which should typically be 90 days, and definitely not more than 12 months

- Marketing/advertising plan to sell the renovated house

- If you are planning to make a business out of this investment strategy, then set up your business as well

- Expected ROI with concrete evidence from experts such as expected market value of the property after renovation, the growth prospects in the chosen location, etc.

Choose the right professionals in the market – You will need expert professionals such as lawyers, realtors, rehabilitation contractors, accountants, and others to make a success of your fix-and-flip investment. Choose your professionals wisely. Connect with many people, speak to them, learn about what they do, read their reviews, and do your homework before deciding on which expert you are going to go with.

Find lenders for your investment plans – If you don't have hard cash for the fix-and-flip investment, then you need to find sound lenders for your project(s). There are primarily three types of lenders who can finance your flipping project(s).

- Hard money loans – You can find plenty of private investors and/or companies who lend money against property security. The approval and processing times are much faster than traditional mortgages. Hard money lenders are more lenient than traditional lenders. However, their interest rates are steeper than the market rates and their loan terms are all for short-term only.

- Rehabilitation loans – Some lenders extend credit lines on existing mortgages which can be used to rehabilitate another project.

- Investment group loans – When you join real estate investor groups, you are likely to find interesting private individuals or groups of people who are willing to lend you money for your rehabilitation project. These kinds of lenders are likely to bet their money on people with successful experience in the fix-and-flip investment market.

Identify the right kind of property for your fix-and-flip strategy – Here are some factors you must consider before closing in on the right property:

- Location – It is wise to choose a property in a location that is close to where you live because you will visit it multiple times during the rehabilitation period.

- Good neighborhood – There is no point in making a home look good if the neighborhood is not well-maintained or is prone to high crime rates and other issues.

- Proximity to amenities – Ensure there are good amenities such as parks, shopping areas, school, and restaurants within reasonable distances from the property.

- Market conditions – Look up the market conditions of the locality and check out how long any property listings of the area were sitting on the market before being sold.

• Structural issues – If the property you choose has structural problems such as poor foundation strength, sinking floors, etc., then not only will your rehab costs go up considerably, you might also need new licenses and permits to complete the renovation. It would be wise, therefore, to avoid properties which have significant structural issues.

• Ensure your repairs add value to the property – Your fix-and-flip properties should ideally get repairs that add value to them. It could be in the form of large closets for increased storage, updated kitchens and bathrooms, and a few cosmetic changes that can give a face-lift to the home. Such value-additions attract buyers.

• Focus on the size of the property – The larger the property, the better for fix-and-flip investment strategy. Alterations to the floor plans, removing load-bearing walls for more room, and other such things can be easily accomplished during the rehabilitation stage. However, you cannot really add new square footage to the property. Therefore, focus on the size when you hunt for fix-and-flip properties.

• Yards and gardens – Again, most buyers would like to see a home with some open space in the form of gardens and yards. You can beautify the space and enhance its appeal as you wish but you cannot add empty space. Therefore, look for properties with this kind of open space.

• After Repair Value (ARV) - The ARV is the estimate of the value of a property after all the repairs, renovations, and rehabilitation works are completed. The ARV will give you a good idea on whether the investment is worth your while or not. To get an accurate idea of the ARV of a property, you need to do the following:

o   Analyze the comparable

o   Calculate all expenses and costs

o   Follow the 70% Rule

Comparables or 'comps' as they are called in the real estate market are recently sold or listed properties that are similar to your investment. Analyze these comps to determine the ARV of your property. This will give you a realistic indication of the worth of your property after repairs and renovations.

Make a detailed listing of all the costs and expenses of the rehabilitation costs. For this, take quotes from reputed contractors. Ensure you check out the quality and deliverance of these professionals. Get estimates for all your materials and ensure you get yourself a good discount for everything. As a beginner, focusing on the budget is, perhaps, the most important aspect of real estate investment.

Once you have the ARV and the expenses and costs involved, follow the 70% rule as follows: (ARV * 0.7) – Rehabilitation costs and expenses. Your cost price of the property should typically not be more than the figure thrown up by this formula.

Mistakes to avoid while investing in fix-and-flip properties – Succeeding in the fix-and-flip market requires a bit more skill and knowledge than the buy-and-hold strategy. Here are some obvious pitfalls that you can avoid to increase your chances for success:

Do not do work for which you are not qualified or trained, especially for skilled work like electrical and plumbing.

Choosing a property that is very far away from where you live. Daily supervision of the renovation work is an essential aspect of the fix-and-flip investment strategy. If you choose a property that is very far away, then a lot of time and energy will be wasted in the travel itself jeopardizing the quality of work and the achievement of time-bound goals.

Spending more than needed for the renovations and rehabilitation works; after all, you are not going to live in the house yourself. Therefore, plan and budget for value-added renovations, and strictly adhere to your planned budget.

As you gain experience in this strategy and build your reputation in the market, you could get investment offers wherein you don't need to put in a penny of your own money in the project.

As your reputation increases in the market driven by your successes, you are likely to find investors who are willing to pay for the entire project while you only handle the operations and get a cut from the final profits. Alternately, lenders might be willing to lend the entire money to you and expect a cut from the equity on the successful sale of the property.

Potential risks in the fix-and-flip strategy – Investors of the fix-and-flip strategy are exposed to the following risks:

- Underestimation of rehabilitation costs

- Holding costs exceeding expectations

- Penalties for extending loan tenures

The longer the rehabilitation work takes, the higher the costs and expenses are going to go. As you will not be able to pay back loans, especially if you have borrowed at high-interest rates from hard money lenders, then your mortgage costs are going to increase too.

Vacation Rentals

Vacation rental properties are homes or houses that are typically bought in tourist destinations. These properties (comparable to Airbnb properties) can serve as a holiday home for you as the investor, and when you are not using it, you can rent the place out to visitors and tourists. For beginners, this might be a great investment option because it gives you the flexibility of using it for yourself as well as renting it out when you don't need it. The vacation rental route is good for:

- People looking for supplemental income.

- People who want to avail of rental tax benefits.

- Beginners because it is one of the simplest ways of getting your foot into the real estate investment market.

- For people who have a favorite place to travel to every year and would like to own a home there with the double benefit of offsetting vacation expenses with homeownership.

Advantages of taking the vacation rentals investment route – Many beginners find the idea of investing in real estate a bit daunting. For such people, vacation rentals could be a great first-step because of the following advantages:

- Dual-purpose property – Clearly, for a new investor, this is a great advantage. You can use this place as a second home when you are on vacation to your favorite place and rent it out when you are not using it.

- Rental income and appreciation – In addition to earning rental income, your property invariably appreciates in value over time, like most other real estate investments.

- Less risky as compared to other real estate investments – The reasons for reduced risks with vacation rentals include:

o   Tourist destinations typically have demand for accommodation, and therefore, you have reduced vacancy risks.

o   Rates are calculated per night-stay thereby letting you earn more faster than with traditional rental income homes.

• It helps you gain hands-on experience with real estate investing – Vacation rentals allow you to be a real estate without being excessively worried about property management, especially if you use the services of vacation rental professionals. Yet, you get first-hand experience on what goes into real estate investments.

You can reduce the risk even further by choosing homes in high-demand tourist destinations. Alternately, you can choose a property that works well as vacation rentals and traditional rental income generators. So, during low occupancy times, you can rent it out as traditional homes. Therefore, when you choose your property wisely, you can switch between being a traditional landlord and an owner of a vacation rental home.

In the worst-case scenario of both these rental options failing (which happens very rarely), you always have the choice of saving money on your holidays by visiting your vacation rental place.

Costs of purchasing vacation rental properties – The following items are typical costs associated with investing in vacation rental properties:

• Lender fees and charges

• Closing costs associated with the mortgage

• Property taxes and insurance

• Cleaning, repairs, and maintenance

• Property management costs

Typically, vacation rental properties bring in higher rents than buy-and-hold properties considering the increased demand for accommodation in tourist places, especially during peak seasons. However, other costs such as regular cleaning and maintenance and insurance are higher too, and the increased rents offset these enhanced costs.

Risks associated with vacation rental properties – These are some of the potential risks you might be exposed to when you choose to invest in vacation rentals:

• Cash flows are typically inconsistent as tenants are seasonal. However, costs such as insurance, taxes, maintenances, etc. are consistent, and you are obliged to pay them irrespective of having or not having tenants. Therefore, you run the risk of being out-of-pocket.

• Vacation rentals are the first set of properties to be negatively impacted during economic downturns.

Real Estate Investment Trusts (REITs)

REITs are companies and trusts that finance, operate, or own income-producing real estate. REITs operate the same way as mutual funds and offer investors to get into the real estate market at low threshold amounts. REITs provide total returns as well as dividend incomes for investors.

As an investor, you can invest in a large portfolio of real estate properties by purchasing stocks, MF units, or through exchange-traded funds (ETFs). The investor earns a share of the income proportional to his or her stock holding. With REITs, you don't need to go out, look up properties, choose what is best for you, etc. Simply invest in the REIT and obtain returns in the form of dividend income and capital appreciation in proportion to the number of stocks or units you hold.

The companies underlying the REITs lease or invest in real estate property, and the income earned from these investments are shared amongst the shareholders and unitholders in the form of dividend income. REITs are mandated to pay out at least 90% of the income earned to shareholders.

How do REITs work? – REITs pay their shareholders from the income they make from real estate investments. A company needs to satisfy the following elements to qualify as a REIT in addition to the other criteria needed to qualify as a trust or company:

• At least 75% of its total assets must be invested in real estate.

• At least 75% of its gross income must come through investments on real estate in the form of rents, mortgage interest, or sale proceeds of property.

• At least 90% of their income should be paid out to investors as dividends each year.

Different categories of REITs – There are many categories of REITs including:

• Equity REITs – Most of the REITs are equity REITs, and just like mutual funds, they invest the pool of money collected from investors in income-producing real estate and share the bulk of the profits (after deducting expenses) as dividends among the shareholders. Primarily, when people mention REITs, they mean equity REITs. Equity REITs are traded on national stock exchanges.

• Mortgage REITs – Referred to as mREITs in short, mortgage REITs investing in real estate by creating or purchasing mortgages or by investing in mortgage-based securities. The interest income earned from these mortgages are shared amongst the shareholders.

• Public Non-Listed REITs – Referred to as PNLRs, the REITs of this category are registered with the Securities and Exchange Commission (SEC) but are not traded on the national stock exchanges. Investments in PNLRs typically a lock-in period and liquidity and redemption are restricted, unlike equity REITs.

- Private REITs – These REITs are not required to be registered with the SEC. They are, of course, not traded on national stock exchanges. Private REITs are generally bought and traded only by institutional investors.

Advantages of investing in REITs – Here are some of the top benefits of investing in REITs:

- Higher dividends – REITs are mandated to pay out at least 90% of their profits to investors resulting in higher dividend yields.

- Professionally managed – REITs are run and managed by experienced professionals in the real estate market ensuring your investors are in the hands of a qualified and robust team of experts. As an individual investor, you might not have the same level of capability to manage high-income-yielding large real estate properties.

- Relatively secured and sustained income – REITs own or manage long-term leases on commercial, residential, and other kinds of properties which can deliver a steady stream of secured rental income for a sustained period of time.

- Portfolio diversification – Real estate and stock markets are generally independent to each other, and they move in opposite directions. Investing in REITs enhances the power of diversification in your overall investment portfolio leading to reduced risks.

- Transparency – REITs are required to be registered with SECs and are subject to regulatory disclosures and other requirements which make these investment companies very transparent.

Disadvantages of investing in REITs – Here are some challenges and disadvantages of investing in REITs:

- Pace of growth is slow – REITs are allowed to reinvest only 10% of their earnings into their real estate businesses because the rest of the money has to be shared amongst the investors. Therefore, most REITs grow at slower paces than other companies.

• Cyclical business of real estate enhances income and stability risks – Income from real estate is cyclical resulting in an inconsistent flow of rental and other forms of income. Downturns in the real estate market could impact the stability of REITs.

• Income from REITs are taxed differently – REITs do not have to pay taxes on profits as 90% of their income is divided amongst investors. However, as an investor, you are required to pay taxes on dividend income from REITs by including it in your personal taxable income. It is not treated as a capital gain. So, if you belong to the higher tax bracket, you end up paying more taxes than if you had invested the money directly in real estate properties.

Crowdfunding Investment Options

Crowdfunding is a new tool wherein real estate businesses raise money for their ventures by leveraging the power of social media platforms such as LinkedIn, Twitter, and Facebook to reach out to an increased number of private individual investors.

Crowdfunding is based on the concept that many people are willing to invest small amounts of money for building a big corpus to be used for development of real estate projects. This approach is a win-win for both investors and real estate businesses. Companies can access investors who were hitherto inaccessible to them, and small-time investors have the opportunity to include real estate elements in their overall investment portfolio.

There are certain rules and regulations to be followed in the crowdfunding segment. For example, investors are screened and classified to check if they are qualified to make investments in the real estate market. Here are some ideas on what to look for and what to know about real estate crowdfunding:

Avoid investing your retirement nest in this space – Although real estate crowdfunding options promise high returns (and some have delivered on their promises), the high-risk-high-reward element in this space is not for your retirement funds. Keep that in capital-protected financial instruments.

Be patient and ready yourself to wait for a long time before you reap the benefits – Experts opine that you must be ready to wait anywhere between 5 and 7 years to begin to see liquidity and visible growth in your investments. So, be prepared for the long haul.

However, there are options wherein you can start earning money within a month of investing in a real estate crowdfunding project. Some companies need quick capital to fulfill last-leg pending orders which means returns on your investment can start sooner than later. You need to do a lot of research to find the right company for your crowdfunding entry into real estate investments.

Look closely at the costs and the expected revenue that the company is promising – If the company is promising something that is too good to be true, then it is time to avoid it. Look for reasonable and sustainable promises that are possible to be delivered. Don't get carried away by offerings of the moon because most scammers build their scamming business on investor naivete.

The company should offer detailed proposals that cover all aspects of the business including potential risks and how it plans to mitigate the risks. Additionally, a good company will include residual risks of their plans as well to let investors know that risks are always part of any business venture. When you see this, you feel confident you are dealing with upright people for whom integrity comes above everything else; a key element for sustained success in the business world.

Look for company reviews – See what earlier investors say about this venture. Are they happy or dissatisfied? Read as many reviews as you can and see what people have to say. Some of the reviews could be biased, so you must learn how to discern between genuine and fake reviews. You can also check the company's track record and see how they have fared in their earlier projects.

Conclusion

Real estate is not just about making quick cash as we have commonly believed—we often assume that people who own or deal with many properties are rich, but this may not be the case all the time. Real estate investing is like investing in any other business—it requires a lot of hard work and determination. The money you get is as a result of getting the right property, using the team you have acquired to make changes to the property at minimal cost, using your community to mobilize buyers, and eventually selling to the right buyer. Real estate largely depends on the relationships that you create, and it is by no means a solo project or career.

The beauty of real estate also lies in its flexibility. Investors can get into it as a one-time gig, but they can also use it to build their lifetime business and wealth. As such, real estate is a source of quick money, but it can also be used to ensure financial freedom and security. While this field does not discriminate against anyone by seeking certification or anything like it, getting into it without the right knowledge could lead to tremendous losses. Because of this, this book is the fountain of knowledge that you need to arm yourself and others around you with information on how to reap the best returns from real estate investing.

Finally, if you found this book useful in any way, a review is always appreciated!